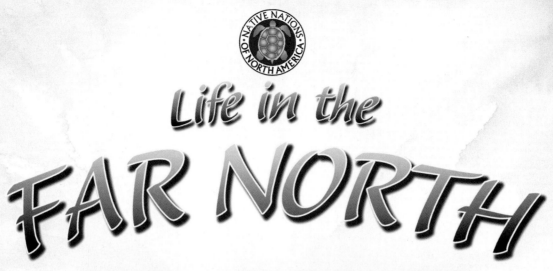

Life in the
FAR NORTH

Bobbie Kalman & Rebecca Sjonger

Crabtree Publishing Company

www.crabtreebooks.com

Created by Bobbie Kalman

Dedicated by Rebecca Sjonger
For my folks, Peter and Doreen Sjonger

Editor-in-Chief
Bobbie Kalman

Writing team
Bobbie Kalman
Rebecca Sjonger

Substantive editor
Niki Walker

Editors
Molly Aloian
Amanda Bishop
Kathryn Smithyman

Art director
Robert MacGregor

Design
Katherine Kantor

Production coordinator
Heather Fitzpatrick

Photo research
Crystal Foxton
Laura Hysert

Consultant
Phyllis Ann Fast,
Associate Professor of
Alaska Native Studies,
University of Alaska Fairbanks

Photographs and reproductions
Reinhard Brucker: page 25 (middle)
Le'on Cogniet, French, 1794-1880. *A Woman from the Land of Eskimos*,
    1826. Oil on canvas, 42.5 x 36.5 cm. c. The Cleveland Museum of
    Art, 2003. Bequest of Noah L. Butkin, 1980.249: page 1
The Granger Collection, New York: page 25 (top)
Greg Harlin, Wood Ronsaville Harlin Inc.: pages 7, 20
© Permission of Lazare & Parker: pages 8, 9, 15, 17, 19, 27
© Permission of Lewis Parker: front cover
National Archives of Canada/1986-35-1: page 29
© SuperStock: pages 16, 30, 31
© West Baffin Eskimo Cooperative, Cape Dorset, Nunavut:
    Young Hunter 1979 Lithograph by Kananginak Pootoogook,
    page 14; *The World Around Me* 1980 Lithograph by Kenojuak
    Ashevak, page 25 (bottom)
W.H. Coverdale Collection of Canadiana/National Archives of
    Canada/1970-188-1271 (detail): page 28
Other images by Digital Vision & Digital Stock

Illustrations
Barbara Bedell: pages 6, 10, 22, 24 (bottom)
Katherine Kantor: border, pages 4, 13 (top), 18, 19, 23 (middle)
Margaret Amy Reiach: pages 5, 12 (top), 13 (middle & bottom), 17, 21,
    23 (top & bottom), 24 (top & middle), 27, and background (pages 1,
    2, 5, 7, 10, 19, 22, 24, 26)
Bonna Rouse: back cover, pages 11, 26
Trevor Morgan: pages 7, 15
Karen Harrison: page 12 (bottom)

Crabtree Publishing Company
www.crabtreebooks.com   1-800-387-7650

PMB 16A
350 Fifth Avenue
Suite 3308
New York, NY
10118

612 Welland Avenue
St. Catharines
Ontario
Canada
L2M 5V6

73 Lime Walk
Headington
Oxford
OX3 7AD
United Kingdom

Cataloging-in-Publication Data
Kalman, Bobbie.
  Life in the far north / Rebecca Sjonger & Bobbie Kalman.
    p. cm. -- (Native nations of North America series)
Includes index.
Summary: Describes the Native nations that have lived for
thousands of years in the northernmost part of present-day
North America, where the frigid climate impacts every aspect of
daily life for such groups as the Init, Yupik, and Inupiat.
  ISBN 0-7787-0377-0 (RLB) -- ISBN 0-7787-0469-6 (pbk.)
  1. Eskimos--Juvenile literature. 2. Arctic regions--Juvenile
literature. [1. Arctic peoples. 2. Arctic regions.] I. Sjonger,
Rebecca. II. Title. III. Series.
E99.E7S5114 2004
971.9004'971--dc22
                                                    2003012911
                                                    LC

Contents

The Far North

The Far North is a vast area of land and water found north of the **Arctic Circle**. It includes the northern parts of Alaska, the Yukon, the Northwest Territories, and Nunavut. Ice covers the ground up to ten months a year. The weather is cold and windy. Temperatures are often below -20°F (-29°C). Even in summer, it is rarely warmer than 50°F (10°C). Despite these conditions, two groups of Native peoples—the Inupiat and the Inuit—have thrived in the Far North for centuries. In the past, they were called **Eskimos**, which means "eaters of raw meat." They prefer the names Inupiat and Inuit, which both mean "the people." The word "Inupiat" is plural, whereas "Inupiaq" describes one person. "Inuit" is used for both plural and singular.

The tree line
When people talk about the Far North or the Arctic, they often mean the area north of the **tree line**. Few trees are found there because their roots cannot grow in the **permafrost**, or frozen soil. The land in the Far North is called the **tundra**.

- - - *Arctic Circle*
tree line
tundra

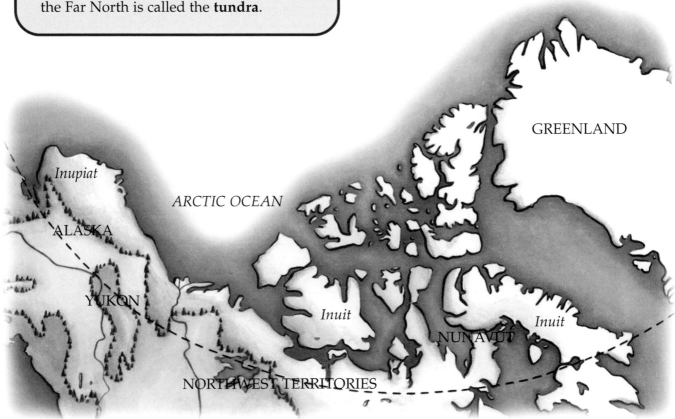

Peoples of the Far North

The Inupiat and the Inuit are **descendants** of the **Thule**. Thule people lived on the northern coast of present-day Alaska around 1,000 years ago. The Thule had many tools and advanced hunting skills. Over time, they spread eastward all the way to present-day Greenland. Many Inupiat and Inuit traditions started with the Thule. This book describes the lives of the Inupiat and the Inuit before people from other lands arrived in the Far North. Inupiat and Inuit groups still live in the region today and carry on many of the traditions described in this book.

The first groups living in the Far North tracked animals across the land.

Relatives in the south

The Inupiat and the Inuit of the Far North are related to the following groups: the Inupiat and the Inuit living south of the Arctic Circle; the Yupiit and the Aleut of Alaska; and the Inuit living in Greenland and Siberia. Their languages all have a common starting point. As the groups split up, huge distances separated them and they began speaking different **dialects**, or versions of the language. The Inupiat dialect is known as **Inupiaq**, whereas the Inuit dialect is called **Inuktitut**. The daily lives of the groups also varied. Yupiit, Aleut, and southern Inupiat and Inuit peoples lived in regions with milder weather than that of the Far North. These groups relied on plants and animals not found north of the tree line.

The Far North's landscape of ice and snow shaped the daily life of the Inupiat and the Inuit.

Family ties

People in the Far North have always worked together to survive in harsh conditions. In the past, families usually traveled, hunted, and lived together. A typical family was made up of a husband, a wife, and two or three children. **Extended families** that included grandparents, aunts, uncles, and cousins often lived close to one another. Aunts and uncles treated their nieces and nephews as their own children, and cousins considered themselves sisters and brothers. Families encouraged males and females over fifteen years of age to marry and start their own families. Relatives were not allowed to marry one another. Sometimes parents arranged suitable marriages, but people were also free to select their own mates. A man and a woman were married when they began living together. If the couple wanted to part ways, they moved to separate homes. Although there were no formal ceremonies, a marriage was a very strong bond with many responsibilities.

Kinship, or family association, was very important. Strangers who entered a village risked being killed if they could not prove they were related to the group living there.

Inupiat villagers

The number of families in one village depended on how much food was available in the area. There was a lot of food in most Inupiat territories, so many extended families lived together in large groups. Some Inupiat villages were home to as many as 1,000 people who were related by blood or by marriage. Relatives living close to one another shared everything, especially during times of hardship. When food became difficult to find, large groups split up to hunt in different areas.

Inuit nomads

The Inuit were **nomadic**. They lived in **camps**, or groups of temporary dwellings, and followed the animals they hunted. In winter, groups of two or three families stayed together. In spring and summer—when finding food was easier—several families formed larger camps.

Leaders

Although men usually made decisions for their families, everyone followed the advice of older family members. All adults respected one another and were treated as equals. On hunting trips, the best hunter or the wisest decision-maker became the leader. Groups that hunted whales turned to the captain of the boat for leadership. **Shamans**, or spiritual leaders, were believed to communicate with spirits, especially those of animals. Shamans were also special healers who used remedies not known to most people.

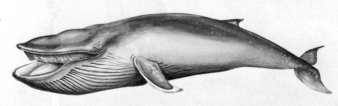

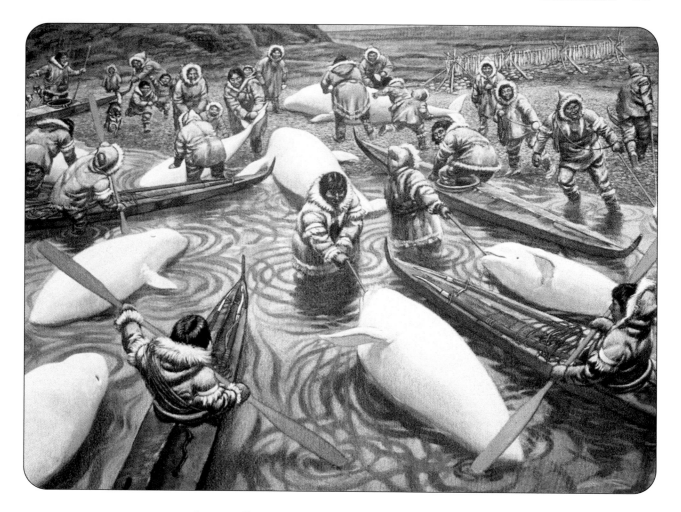

Roles and duties

Every member of a community had specific roles and duties to ensure there was enough food, shelter, and clothing. Even young children helped out. Men and women had different tasks, but these duties were equally important.

Men and boys

Men and older boys had many duties, including hunting, fishing, making tools, and trading. A good hunting or fishing trip provided a family with food as well as materials needed for building shelters and for making clothing and tools. During the long winter months, men worked inside, making and repairing weapons and tools. At different times throughout the year, they traded goods and natural materials with men from other regions. They met to trade for things that were rare in their own areas. **Coastal dwellers**, for example, had sea oil to trade, whereas **inland dwellers** had extra caribou hides to exchange. The Inupiat had very strict rules about which goods could be traded and with whom.

Women and girls

Women and girls had many tasks, such as taking care of their homes, **preserving** and preparing food, and making clothing. They cleaned fish and cut up meat for food, which was rarely cooked. Raw fish and meat froze in the cold temperatures and could be stored for months. In summer, women and girls gathered berries and plants that they dried and saved for winter. Women also learned how to heal people using herbs and gave medical care to their families.

Making clothes

Women and girls prepared animal hides to sew them into clothing. They removed an animal's hide with a knife, scraped the hide clean, and soaked it in water. The damp hide was then stretched either by hand or on frames. Finally, the prepared hides were cut and sewn into clothing. Women used small, neat stitches to make clothes windproof and waterproof.

Although most people today buy their clothes, the traditional process is still used to make clothing.

Children's lives

Inupiat and Inuit parents have always valued
their children. In the past, many families had
only one or two children. Mothers were the main
caregivers, but fathers also took part in bringing
up their sons and daughters. Parents encouraged
their children to be patient and cheerful. The
children were also expected to work hard,
share their belongings with others, and learn
the names and histories of all their relatives.

Keeping babies close
Mothers carried their babies with
them everywhere they went. Infants
were nestled in their mothers' warm
amauti, which were the large hoods
attached to women's **parkas**, or coats.
With their babies so close, mothers
were able to tend to their needs easily
throughout the day. Children
stayed in these hoods
until they were
old enough
to walk.

*When babies were born, they were usually
named after relatives who had died recently.
The names of grandparents were often
given to newborns.*

Time to play

Children were free to roam anywhere in their villages or camps because strangers were not permitted to enter. They often played with toy versions of the tools and weapons used by their parents. Adults crafted items such as miniature harpoons, sleds, and oil lamps to help children learn adult tasks.

Helping hands

Inupiat and Inuit parents wanted their children to become strong, healthy adults. Children who grew up and started their own families were expected to care for their elderly relatives. During times when food was hard to find, families with extra food adopted the children of people—usually from their extended families—who did not have enough to eat.

Growing up

Mothers and fathers taught their children the skills they would need to provide for their own families one day. When boys turned five years old, they began helping their fathers with duties such as building the family home. Fathers also taught their sons the important skill of carving. At seven years of age, girls started helping their mothers with household duties such as preparing food or making and mending clothing. Girls also looked after younger children. Children learned to be obedient and to respect the authority of their elders, but they were rarely punished.

By the age of ten, boys were taken on their first fishing or hunting trip.

Materials from nature

The Inupiat and the Inuit living north of the tree line had few trees to use for wood. Although plants grew in spring and summer, they were not plentiful. There were, however, many other **natural resources**, or useful materials available in nature. Inupiat and Inuit groups were very creative in using whatever resources were available. Animals were especially important to their survival. People hunted fish, seals, whales, narwhals, walruses, polar bears, caribou, rabbits, and birds. They found uses for almost every part of the animals. Animal meat and blood were the main sources of food. Animal hides and furs were fashioned into clothing, shelters, containers, and many other household items. People used seal oil and **blubber**, or whale fat, as both fuel and food. Seal stomachs and **intestines** were turned into waterproof sacks and coats. Emptied stomachs were blown up to make fishing floats that were attached to spears. Bones, **ivory**, claws, and antlers were used to make most weapons and tools. Sometimes Inupiat and Inuit groups made long trips in search of supplies.

fishing float attached to spear

Some Inupiat relied on bowhead whales for their survival. These whales were the main source of food, fuel, and building supplies.

Sticks and stones

Since there were so few trees, wood was very valuable. People collected **driftwood** they found floating along the coastlines. It was saved to build shelters or to carve into masks, tools, and sleds. Stones and rocks also had many uses in the Far North. People could carve and shape them into tools such as knives and weapons such as harpoon points. Flat rocks were stacked to make an **inukshuk**, which was a human-shaped statue. Inuit in present-day Canada built these structures to mark routes and hunting spots.

An inukshuk built in the path of a caribou herd helped redirect the animals to nearby hunters.

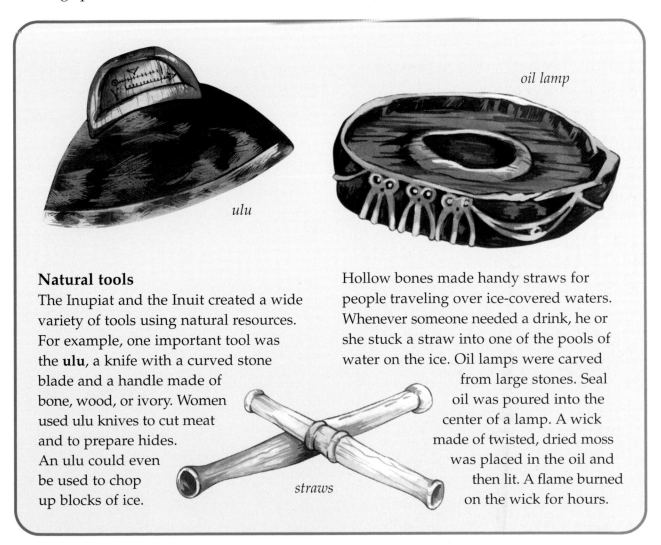

oil lamp

ulu

straws

Natural tools

The Inupiat and the Inuit created a wide variety of tools using natural resources. For example, one important tool was the **ulu**, a knife with a curved stone blade and a handle made of bone, wood, or ivory. Women used ulu knives to cut meat and to prepare hides. An ulu could even be used to chop up blocks of ice.

Hollow bones made handy straws for people traveling over ice-covered waters. Whenever someone needed a drink, he or she stuck a straw into one of the pools of water on the ice. Oil lamps were carved from large stones. Seal oil was poured into the center of a lamp. A wick made of twisted, dried moss was placed in the oil and then lit. A flame burned on the wick for hours.

Hunting and fishing

The Inupiat and the Inuit depended on hunting and fishing for food and supplies. Although some animals **migrated**, or traveled long distances, through the region, people knew when and where to find them. They tracked many types of animals.

Land and ocean animals

The kinds of animals a group hunted depended on where the people lived. Inland dwellers hunted land animals including caribou, foxes, and rabbits. They also caught fish, such as trout, from lakes and rivers. People living along the coasts changed their hunting and fishing patterns with the seasons. In winter, coastal dwellers hunted animals such as polar bears, which lived on the thick ice that covered the ocean. When

the ice thawed in summer, coastal peoples caught fish such as halibut and hunted seals, walruses, and sea lions. Right whales, bowhead whales, and humpback whales were hunted along the coast during spring and summer. Some groups also moved inland to catch freshwater fish and hunt land animals.

Respect for animals

The peoples of the Far North believed that each animal had a spirit. Before a hunt, they performed ceremonies and sang sacred songs to encourage animals to sacrifice their lives. After a successful hunting trip, people offered thanks and gifts to the spirits of the animals that were killed. For example, they gave offerings of fresh water to satisfy the spirits of ocean animals such as whales.

Skill and patience

Hunting required a great deal of skill and could be dangerous. The catches were often larger than the boats used by hunters and fishers! Men risked their lives to hunt. If their boats flipped, they could die in the icy water. Hunters also had to be patient. Some spent hours on the ice, waiting for animals, such as seals, to pop up through holes for air. Hunters had to be ready to strike at any moment.

Expert whalers

The coastal Inupiat were excellent **whalers**, or whale hunters. They used Thule weapons, such as harpoons, and large whaling boats called **umiaks** (see page 17). These boats made hunting huge whales less dangerous. Whalers did not have to move as often as nomadic hunters did. A single large whale provided food and supplies for many families. If enough of the whale was preserved, people did not have to seek more food for the rest of the year. The small beluga whales found in the Inuit territories of present-day Canada fed far fewer people.

Seals were common sources of food, fuel, and hides.

Over land and sea

The Native peoples of the Far North were—and still are—experts at traveling on land, ice, and water. In the past, the Inupiat and the Inuit had various ways to cover long distances. The transportation they used depended on the purpose of the trip and the route they took. Sometimes walking was the easiest way to travel over land or ice. At other times, people used sleds. Boats transported people along waterways. Many boats and sleds used today still have traditional designs.

When traveling long distances, people often rode in the sleds with their belongings.

Sleds and dog teams

When people traveled across snow and ice to hunt or to move to new areas, they often carried many items with them. The fastest and easiest way to travel was by sled. Some sleds were up to sixteen feet (5 m) long. To make a sled, people attached **runners** made of bones, driftwood, or even frozen fish to the bottom of a platform shaped from bone or driftwood. Water was poured on the runners to make them icy and slick. A team of up to fourteen trained husky dogs were attached to a sled with harnesses. The powerful dog team could pull a heavily loaded sled. Husky dogs were useful on hunting trips for many reasons, including their ability to track the scents of land animals.

Kayaks

Kayaks were small, covered one- or two-person boats. They allowed hunters to paddle quickly and quietly through icy waters, as shown below. A kayak was also very light and easy to carry over land. It was made of sealskin or caribou hides stretched over a driftwood frame. The hides were waterproofed first with seal oil. One or two small openings—each just big enough to fit one person—were left in the top of the boat's covering. The kayak's snug shape was designed to keep out cold water and protect the kayaker. If the kayak ever tipped, it could be righted fairly easily.

Umiaks

Umiaks were much larger than kayaks. An umiak looked like an oversized rowboat and could carry up to twenty people or a large load of goods. Whereas kayaks were used in icy coastal waters, umiaks were made for the open ocean. Whalers used these boats to track and surround whales. To construct a watertight umiak, builders used walrus hides waterproofed with seal oil. They stretched the hides over a frame made of whale bones. Later umiaks also had masts and sails.

umiak

Shelters

The Inupiat and the Inuit built various kinds of shelters. The type of dwelling people built depended on the weather, on how long they would use the shelter, and on the available materials. Most structures could be assembled very quickly. When it was time to move on, some people saved the materials they used to make their dwelling, such as driftwood or hides, and carried them to new sites.

Sod houses

Until the early 1900s, the **sod house** was the most common type of home built by the Inupiat and the western Inuit. Sod houses were used during the winter months. They were formed by building a driftwood or whalebone frame over a hollow in the ground. Layers of stones and earth placed on top of the frame made the house look like a small hill from the outside. Being partly underground kept out cold winds and made the sod house interior warm. Some people left their sod houses in spring, when the ground started to thaw and the floors became soggy. Many families came back to the same sod houses every fall.

Qargit

Groups of extended families often built community sod houses, which were called **qargit**. Qargit were larger than regular sod houses. They were used as places for men to gather and socialize and to perform ceremonies. During the dark winter days, men may also have used their qargit as indoor workshops in which they constructed new boats and repaired older boats.

If one family left its sod house to travel to another area, other families were welcome to stay in it.

Snow houses

In winter, the central and eastern Inuit usually lived in dome-shaped snow houses, called **igluvigak**. Igluvigak were often built along coastlines in areas sheltered by cliffs. Travelers camped in smaller snow houses. Two people could build a snow shelter in just a few hours. After marking out a circle where the snow house would be built, they cut blocks of hard, packed snow with an ivory snow saw. They layered row upon row of blocks on the circle, creating a dome. The curved walls were stronger than straight walls against winds. Large snow houses built by a community were called **qaggiq**.

snow saw

Tents

During the short springs and summers, many coastal dwellers traveled inland in search of plants and animals. They carried sealskins or the hides of caribou from camp to camp to use as tents. Although the shapes of tents differed from region to region, they were all made by placing hides over poles. Strong tent poles were made of bones, antlers, or driftwood. People often hung their supplies from the ends of the poles. Heavy rocks were placed along the bottom of the hides to keep the tent from flapping in the wind. People who lived in southern areas could live in tents all year.

19

Inside the home

Sod houses and snow houses looked different on the outside, but the insides of these homes were surprisingly similar. Both shelters kept people very comfortable, even in the coldest, windiest weather. Families spent the long winter months working and playing in their cozy homes.

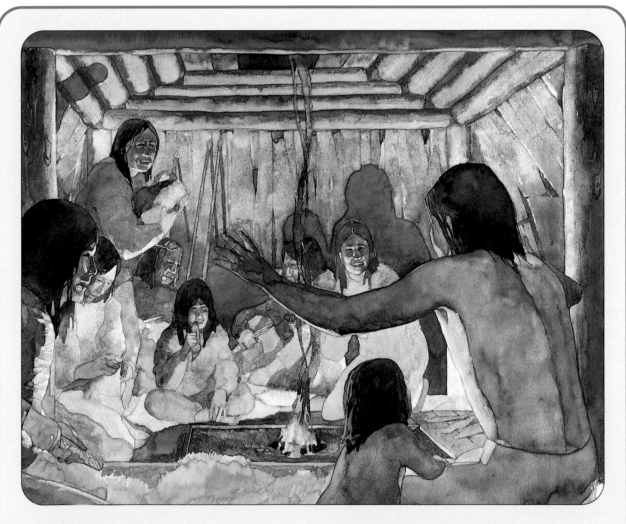

Inside a sod house

Families often returned to the same sod houses year after year. The interiors of these homes were comfortable and well organized. People laid driftwood and stones over the dirt floors and placed animal hides on top of them. They also hung furs on the walls to add warmth. Thin animal intestines were stretched into panels and then used as windows.

20

Inside a snow house

Although snow houses were made of a cold material, their interiors were very warm. To keep out cold winds, people sealed the cracks between the snow blocks by holding an oil lamp up to the interior walls. The blocks melted slightly, but quickly refroze into a solid sheet of ice. Sunlight shone through the ice and lit up the inside of the home. The walls and floors of the snow house were covered with animal hides and furs.

Raised platforms of snow provided places for working, eating, and sleeping.

Tunnels

The entrances to sod houses and snow houses were often reached through tunnels, which helped keep cold winds from blowing into the homes. A sod house tunnel was dug into the earth, whereas a snow house tunnel was dug through the snow. Animal hides were hung in the doorway to keep warm air from escaping. Tunnels also connected separate living, sleeping, and storage areas.

Keeping warm

Wood was so scarce that people rarely burned it. Instead, oil lamps provided heat and light. Racks crafted from driftwood hung well above the lamps. Wet clothing was placed on the racks, where the warmth of the flame dried them. A hole was made in the roof to allow smoke to escape.

A good night's sleep

Both sod houses and snow houses had raised sleeping platforms. Warm air was trapped against the ceiling, so people lying on a platform stayed warm as they slept. A sod house platform was made of driftwood covered in furs. A snow house platform was carved from snow and covered with a layer of wooden objects such as paddles. Next, moss and furs were arranged over the wooden layer. Fur clothing was folded to use as pillows. Younger members of the family sometimes slept on the floor.

Clothing

Warm, waterproof clothing was essential in the Far North. It was made from caribou, seal, polar bear, wolf, fox, and squirrel hides and fur. Women used animal **sinew**, or strong connective tissue, to sew the hides together. People wore several layers of clothing for warmth. The fur on the inner layer was worn against the body to trap heat. The fur on the outer layer faced outward to keep out cold.

Keeping dry

People took great care to keep their clothing dry because wet hides became stiff and uncomfortable. Before entering their homes, they used special sticks to beat wet snow off parkas and pants. Inside, they took off their damp clothes and hung them up to dry. To keep hide clothing comfortable, women chewed the hides after they dried. Sometimes seal intestines were cleaned and sewn into an outer waterproof layer of clothing.

Early explorers thought the peoples of the Far North were very fat! Layers of clothing made their bodies look much larger than they really were.

Men's and women's clothing

Men and women wore similar clothes. Hooded parkas shielded them from freezing winds. Hoods were often lined with wolf fur, which did not freeze easily. Warm, waterproof pants were tucked into boots to keep out snow. Mittens were made of fur, with the fur worn against the hands. They were attached to each other with a string so they did not get separated or lost.

Children's clothing

Babies often wore only diapers because their mothers' amauti kept them warm. Diapers were made of moss or hide. Children started to wear clothing when they learned to walk. Their first clothes were one-piece outfits made of sealskin or caribou hide. Older children wore the same styles of clothing as those of their parents.

Special decoration

Ceremonial clothing was decorated with ivory, feathers, beads, and animal furs and tails. People also attached **amulets**, or small charms, to their clothes. Amulets were believed to bring good luck and safety from harm. They were made from a variety of natural materials such as animal bones and claws. Earrings, nose rings, lip plugs, and other types of jewelry were made from shells, stones, ivory, or wood. Depending on local customs, some young women had their faces tattooed.

Snow goggles carved from ivory or driftwood protected people's eyes from the wind and the glare of the sun on snow.

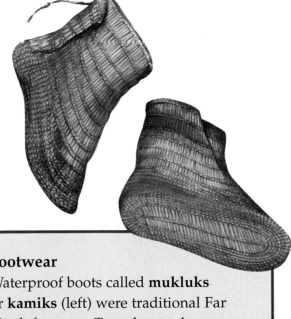

Footwear

Waterproof boots called **mukluks** or **kamiks** (left) were traditional Far North footwear. To make sturdy, warm boots, moss or feathers were stuffed between layers of caribou hide or sealskin. Men's boots were usually knee high. Women's boots were taller, often reaching the middle of the thigh. Inside the boots, socks or stockings protected the feet. Long grasses that grew during the brief summer were braided into snug socks (above). Soft, thin animal hides were crafted into cozy stockings that were worn in winter.

Arts

The Inupiat and the Inuit created everyday items that were both useful and attractive. Men carved ivory, bone, antlers, and driftwood into containers, utensils, fishing gear, knife handles, and weapons. They considered the natural shape of the material before deciding what to carve. Practical objects such as combs or needle holders were decorated with beautiful carvings of birds, marine and land animals, and human forms.

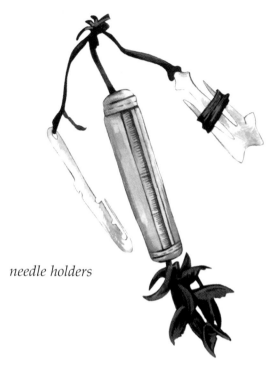

needle holders

Although the Inupiat and the Inuit of the past made beautiful objects, their language had no word for "art."

Bow drills

The **bow drill** is a traditional carving tool. It is made up of a long bone with a pointed end attached to a bone-and-sinew bow. The carver keeps one end of the long, pointed bone steady with his teeth. Holding the piece of art in one hand, the carver uses the other hand to move the bow quickly back and forth. Moving the bow causes the bone to spin and cut into the artwork.

Some Native artists continue to carve with traditional bow drills.

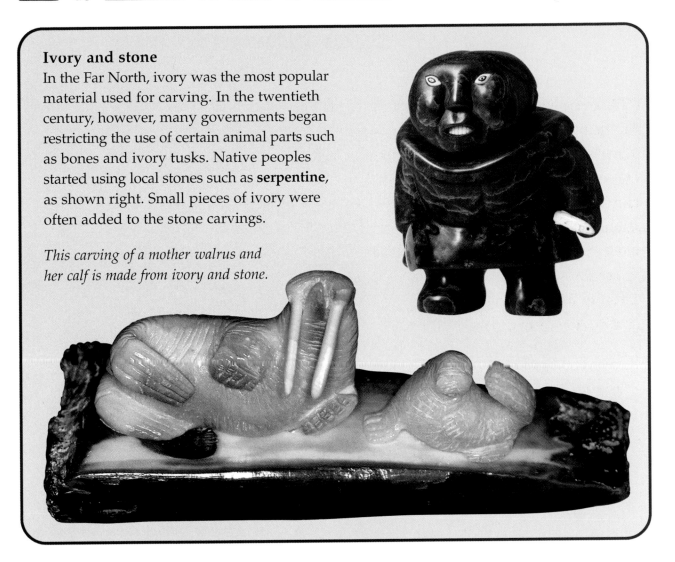

Ivory and stone

In the Far North, ivory was the most popular material used for carving. In the twentieth century, however, many governments began restricting the use of certain animal parts such as bones and ivory tusks. Native peoples started using local stones such as **serpentine**, as shown right. Small pieces of ivory were often added to the stone carvings.

This carving of a mother walrus and her calf is made from ivory and stone.

Modern art

In the late 1800s, artwork began to change. European and Russian newcomers wanted Inupiat and Inuit art to take home with them, so Native carvers began creating pieces to sell. Instead of traditional themes from nature, which were meant to honor animals and spirits, the new art was based on European designs. Today, Inupiat and Inuit artists use modern subjects and techniques as well as creating traditional artworks.

Modern artworks celebrate Inupiat or Inuit culture, using materials such as colored pencils or watercolors.

Fun and games

The Inupiat and the Inuit worked hard year-round, but people were busiest during the short summers. People spent as much time as possible working outside in the sunshine and warm weather. Although there was work to do during winter, people had much more free time. During long, dark winter days, older people told stories, which they had learned over many years from their parents and grandparents. Through these stories, children learned the histories and spiritual beliefs of their people. Some tales went on for so long that everyone was asleep by the time they ended!

Getting active

There were many active ways to spend spare time. The oldest games, such as wrestling matches, jumping games, and running races, tested the strength and ability of the participants and helped people stay in shape. These games did not need any equipment. Far North versions of kickball and juggling were also popular. Players used various types of balls made with animal hides and fur stuffing. **Blanket tossing** (above) was—and still is—a fun event for a large gathering. A group holds a sealskin or walrus hide in the air by its edges, creating a bouncy surface on which to jump. People then take turns jumping on it. The winner is the person who jumps the highest.

Hunting practice

Boys and men often played games using hunting weapons to practice their skills. For example, there were many games played with a **bola**. A bola was made from strings of sinew attached to bone discs. When it was thrown in hunting, the bola wrapped around an animal's legs or a bird's wings. Bola games often involved hitting a hanging target.

Indoor games

Many indoor games were enjoyed by the whole family. Ring-and-pin games, bone puzzles, and string games were common pastimes. In the ring-and-pin game shown right, a hole was drilled into a large piece of bone. It was attached to a bone spike with a cord of sinew. The goal was to toss the large bone into the air and catch it with the spike.

Group celebrations

People enjoyed yearly celebrations, which were linked to spiritual ceremonies or to the changing of the seasons. They gathered together in their community qargit or qaggiq and spent many hours singing, dancing, drumming, storytelling, and sharing huge meals.

Ring-and-pin games are popular all over the world.

Outsiders arrive

In the 1500s, some coastal Inuit groups were briefly visited by British explorers who were searching for new sailing routes to Asia. The explorers found life in the tundra too challenging. They did not stay long, but before they left, some of these newcomers kidnapped Native people to put on display in Europe. **Settlers** did not arrive in the Far North until the early 1700s—much later than in other places in North America. Over time, however, more and more Europeans and Russians came to search for natural resources.

The newcomers soon discovered that the Inupiat and the Inuit were excellent hunters and fishers and quickly began to take advantage of their skills and knowledge. Europeans and Russians offered the Native groups packaged foods, metal tools and weapons, and household items. Inupiat and Inuit peoples came to depend on these goods and were forced to hunt and fish to trade for them. In the 1700s, Inupiat whalers were encouraged to work with foreign whaling teams that wanted to kill as many whales as possible. The number of bowhead whales quickly declined. In the mid-1800s, **fur traders**, or people who exchanged goods for furs, came to the Far North and began deciding which animals would be hunted. Animals were hunted only for their valuable furs. Their meat and body parts were wasted. Over time, many of the traditional ways of peoples in the Far North were replaced by new ways.

New beliefs

The newcomers also tried to change the spiritual beliefs of the Inupiat and the Inuit. **Missionaries** offered new forms of health care and education to the Native peoples. In exchange, the missionaries expected the people to reject their ancient beliefs and become Christians. Some Inupiat and Inuit peoples combined this new religion with their old ways. Others refused to change their beliefs and were harshly treated as a result.

Broken trust

The people who took over Inupiat and Inuit lands did not respect nature in the way the Native groups did. The Europeans and Russians forced their own trade and religious systems on the Inupiat and the Inuit, which led to the loss of traditional ways of life. The newcomers also brought infectious diseases, such as influenza, measles, and smallpox, which the Inupiat and the Inuit had never encountered before. Their bodies had no natural defenses against the new illnesses. As a result, entire families became very sick and died. Many Inupiat and Inuit developed a strong distrust of the people who caused the destruction of their communities and their traditions.

Life in the Far North today

In the 1900s, the governments of the United States and Canada imposed laws and restrictions on the peoples of the Far North. The governments built new communities and encouraged the Inupiat and the Inuit to settle in them. It was difficult for the Native peoples to maintain their old ways of life in these new communities. The governments also sent many children to **residential schools**, where they were not allowed to use their languages or practice traditional ways. Today, Inupiat and Inuit peoples work hard to keep their languages and traditions alive. Children are taught to read, write, and speak Inupiaq and Inuktitut, which connects them to their peoples' pasts.

Modern schools, hospitals, stores, churches, and sports centers make northern towns look just like those found in other parts of the United States and Canada. Inupiat and Inuit communities hold many reminders of the past, however. Some new homes have designs similar to those used hundreds of years ago in snow houses. Although modern fabrics and designs are common, traditional clothing remains the warmest choice for people who live in the Far North. Sleds, kayaks, and umiaks are still used for travel. Snowmobiles, however, make it fast and easy to travel short distances. Airplanes carry people, food, and supplies to remote areas in the Far North.

Reclaiming lands

In the mid-1900s, many Native peoples began demanding the right to live in the traditional way. The Inuit Circumpolar Conference was established in 1977 to promote the unity and development of peoples living in Alaska, Canada, Greenland, and Russia. Native groups throughout North America, including the peoples of the Far North, have taken governments to court to reclaim their lands. In 1999, the Government of Canada settled a claim with the Inuit and created a 770,000 square mile (2 million km²) territory called Nunavut. "Nunavut" means "our land" in Inuktitut. The creation of Nunavut was a major victory for the Inuit of Canada.

Visit these interesting websites to learn more about life in the Far North today as well as in the past:
- www.allthingsarctic.com/people/index.htm
- www.alaskanative.net
- www.kstrom.net/isk/canada/images/can_arct.htm

Today, snowmobiles are more likely to pull sleds than dog teams are.

Glossary

Note: Boldfaced words that are defined in the book may not appear in the glossary

Arctic Circle Line of latitude at 66° north

coastal dweller A person who lives along the shore where ocean meets land

descendant A person who comes from a particular ancestor or group of ancestors

driftwood Wood that is carried by a body of water from one shore to another shore

inland dweller A person who lives in the interior of a region, away from the ocean

intestines Tubes in an animal's body that carry wastes away from its stomach

Inuktitut The dialect used by the Inuit

Inupiaq The dialect used by the Inupiat; describing an individual

ivory An off-white material that forms the tusks of a mammal

missionary A person who tries to convert people to a different religion

nomadic Describing a lifestyle in which people move from one location to the next, following the animals they hunt

preserve To prepare a food so it does not spoil

residential school A government-run school that forced Native children to give up their traditional ways and learn American or Canadian customs

runner A long, thin support on which a sled slides

settler A person who moves to a new place and makes it his or her home

tree line The northern point where trees become stunted or do not grow at all because of permanently frozen ground

Index

1 2 3 4 5 6 7 8 9 0 Printed in the U.S.A. 3 2 1 0 9 8 7 6 5 4